THE 30-DAY DEVOTIONAL
BOOK FOR YOUNG ADULTS:

30 DEVOTIONS, 30 AUTHORS, 30 TOPICS

Edited and Published by:
Courtney A. Jacobs

THE 30-DAY DEVOTIONAL BOOK FOR YOUNG ADULTS: 30 DEVOTIONS, 30 AUTHORS, 30 TOPICS

Cover and interior design by ThiruMoolar Devar

Print ISBN: 979-8-9859495-0-6

eBook ISBN: 979-8-9859495-1-3

I want to first off thank my Lord and Savior Jesus Christ for giving me the vision for this book. I want to thank my number one fan, my mother Dr. Jacqueline Jacobs, and my aunt Nicole Barnett for helping me throughout this entire process. Last but not least, thanks to all the authors that helped me complete this vision. I literally could not have done this without any of you:

Ernestine Barnett

Nicole & Jeff Barnett

Gloria J. Bell

Amber Booze-Graham

Lenae Brooks

Jillian Causey

Amber Chapman

Dr. Artelia M. Covington

Jacara Davis

Ray Dugga

Dr. Prince Frimpong

Dr. David W. Gadson

Dr. Shalena Heard

Valerie Henson

Dr. Jacqueline Jacobs

Courtney Jacobs

Andrea Jones

Dara Jones

Willie Mull

Victoria Nicole

Josh Parker

Valerie Parker

Janis Perry

Jeremy Perry

Renee Perry Leech

Jed Pilgrim

Judith K. Vanderhoof, M.A., LCPC

Collin Savage

Pastor Irving Clark II

*From *'One of Them: Bringing Bold Faith to a Broken World'* by Jonathan and Lenia Queen

Table of Contents

DAY 1:
The Grip of Anxiety

Philippians 4:6-7 (NLT)

"Don't worry about anything; instead, pray about everything. Tell God what you need, and thank him for all he has done. Then you will experience God's peace, which exceeds anything we can understand. His peace will guard your hearts and minds as you live in Christ Jesus."

Anxiety. That gut-wrenching, panic-stricken feeling. You know, the one where fear invades, you can't sleep, can't eat, and your body is so tense, it feels like an out-of-body experience.

If you have never experienced the grip of anxiety, lucky you! As for the rest of us, anxiety feels never-ending. Not only are we battling our thoughts, doubts, and insecurities, but we're impacted by social media, TV, movies, and reading. If we're not careful, we find ourselves stuck in this cycle, under a haze of cloudy thinking, making us ask, "Are You There God? It's Me."

I know how you feel. A few years ago, anxiety gripped me so badly. Every day I felt like a zombie. I would wake up, wishing to be asleep. God felt so far away. I started to believe that God was anywhere but in my situation.

You see for me, anxiety stems from worry. When our minds begin to overanalyze about our current plight, or the future, playing out every scenario in our head, eventually anxiety sets in and disrupts our peace.

Despite that, I have good news for you! All of that anxiousness, worry, and fear – we don't have to let it consume us. Jesus tells you to "let not your heart be troubled" (John 14: 27 NKJV). While we can't stop worry from coming, as believers, we have the power of the Holy Spirit to let anxiety not control us. We are not defenseless in our fight!

Take another look at Philippians 4:6-7; God tells us not to worry about ANYTHING. That means absolutely NOTHING. Even that thing. Yes, THAT thing. The thing you don't think God can handle. The thing that God has taken too long to work out. The thing that has hurt you so badly, He says you don't worry, not even a little. You might say, that sounds great, but HOW can I not worry?

Well, we don't have to worry because Jesus knows what we need. See, Jesus was there in the beginning, so he already knows the end. He knew every moment, every worry, every fear, every anxious thought you'd have, and he still says you don't worry. Why? Because he can and will handle anything.

What always gets me about this passage is that Jesus doesn't just say 'don't worry'; he says instead to ask him for what we need and then to thank him! Now, if I'm being honest, I'm not thinking about thanking Jesus when I'm panicky and stressed out! Nonetheless then I'm reminded of what the word says in 2 Chronicles 20:22 (as well as the great prophet Marvin Sapp): praise confuses the enemy. This verse means that when we praise God despite of our feelings, emotions, or situation, the enemy doesn't understand. When we confuse the enemy, he realizes you know something he already knows – he can't have you. He can't have your praise or your joy. He realizes you understand your feelings don't control you, and then he flees.

When we do what God asks, we have His peace. The robust and secure peace surrounds us, captivates us, protects us, and sustains us.

I know it's hard and I know anxiety feels too powerful, but you CAN overcome anxiety! You will live and be victorious because our Savior is with you!

DAY 2:
Step out with Courage

- Joshua 1:1-3 (NIV)

God Installed Joshua as Leader

After the death of Moses the servant of the LORD, the LORD said to Joshua son of Nun, Moses' aide: ² "Moses my servant is dead. Now then, you and all these people, get ready to cross the Jordan River into the land I am about to give to them. ³ I will give you every place where you set your foot, as I promised Moses

Read: Joshua 1:1-18, Numbers 13:1-33

On so many occasions, we allow ourselves to be engulfed by fear and turn to lose every strength and all courage, even when we can see and smell the victory. God, through Moses, dispatched Joshua (Hoshea), the son of Nun, and eleven other leaders of Israel to go and spy the land of Canaan. These leaders completed the assignment. They brought home every good evidence and said the "land to which you sent us, and it does flow with milk and honey," and yet, ten of the leaders saw themselves as grasshoppers (Numbers 13:1-33). With this type of "grasshopper mentality," we will always be self-defeated and will not be able to achieve any victory.

Now Joshua, who joined Caleb and showed courage to "go up and take possession of the land" (Numbers 13:30), received his personal marching orders from God to lead Israel to possess the land of Canaan. God promised Joshua, "I will give you every place where you set your foot" (Joshua 1:3-4); "No one will be able to stand against you all the days of your life" (Joshua 1:5a); "I will be with you" (Joshua 1:5b); "I will never leave you" (Joshua 1:5c).

However, in addition to these beautiful and powerful promises, God expected Joshua to show strength and courage in his assignments (Joshua 1:6-7). At the same time he kept His Word and meditated on it to achieve His victories, success, and prosperity (Joshua 1:8). Was it easy for Joshua to carry on the assignments? Not so fast. God continued to remind Joshua what was expected of him. In Joshua 1:9, God said to Joshua, "Have I not commanded you? Be strong and courageous. Do not be afraid; do not be discouraged, for the LORD your God will be with you wherever you go."

God in Christ Jesus has promised us that "He will never leave us or forsake us" (Hebrews 13:5), but when we face reality, "when the rubber meets the road," our strength and courage evaporate, and we tend to lose sight of our God and Savior. We then become like "grasshoppers in our own eyes" (Numbers 13:33), and the challenge maximizes itself. How often do we throw in the towel before the whistle is blown to face the challenge? How often do we forget the promise that "God will never leave us or forsake us" (Hebrews 13:5)? How often do we forget that "we are complete in Christ Jesus in whom the fullness of the Godhead lives in bodily form?" (Colossians 2:9-10). What did we do with the call, "Come unto me, all ye that labor and are heavy laden, and I will give you rest?" (Matthew 11:28). It is time to muster courage and strength to step out to claim the victories He has won for us. Step out with courage to possess your possessions (Joshua 23:5).

As Reinhold Neibuhr (1892-1971), in his serenity prayer, cries out,

"God grant me the serenity to accept the things I cannot change;

Courage to change the things I can; and wisdom to know the difference."

Prayer:

Father, help us muster courage and strength to step out in faith with you to take hold of the victories you have won for us in Christ Jesus. Amen.

DAY 3:
5 W's and H for Discernment

It is essential that you pray and ask the Lord for a discerning spirit. This goes back to the basic "why, when, who, etc." questions. Our thoughts can misguide us and cause us to make the wrong decisions. The only way you will do what is right is to trust the Holy Spirit who lives within you to guide you. This is one of the purposes of the Holy Spirit – to guide us. Jesus told his disciples that He was leaving, but he would send another to be with us. The one that He referred to is the Holy Spirit! Listen to Him when something does not sound or feel right, and trust that it is He who is guiding you.

John 14:15-18, NKJV: "If you love Me, keep My commandments. And I will pray the Father, and He will give you another Helper, that He may abide with you forever— the Spirit of truth, whom the world cannot receive, because it neither sees Him nor knows Him; but you know Him, for He dwells with you and will be in you. [18] I will not leave you orphans; I will come to you."

WHO you are -- Child of God.

WHAT - you have been taught.

WHEN - you are facing adversities, pray for direction and **ask Him to speak to your heart.**

WHERE - your thoughts should be on a direction.

WHY - because you were created on purpose for a purpose.

HOW- eliminate distractions, be still and listen for God's voice.

DAY 4:
Drop Your Weapon

Quotation-

Then the scribes and Pharisees brought to Him a woman caught in adultery. And when they had set her in the midst, they said to Him, "Teacher, this woman was caught in adultery, in the very act. Now Moses, in the law, commanded us that such should be stoned. But what do You say?" John 8:3-5 NKJV

Revelation-

So when they continued asking Him, He raised Himself up and said to **them**, "He who is without sin among you, let him throw a stone at her first."

And again He stooped down and wrote on the ground.

Inspiration-

When you are one of them, Jesus will stop you from judging and criticizing someone you intend to hurt, who instead, needs to be forgiven.

The setting is a beautiful evening wedding. The church is adorned with low lit candles, bright flowers and lavish decorations. There is excitement and expectation in the air. Finally, the moment everyone has been waiting for arrives. The organist plays softly, everyone stands to their feet and the bride begins her entrance.

You would expect to see smiles and hear oohs and ahhs, but not in this case. The faces around the church are filled with disgust and disdain. Before the bride makes it halfway down the aisle, a man yells out "I object to this marriage!" A lady behind him nods in agreement. "Me too, she is a whore!"

There are more nods of agreement. No one in the crowd disagrees or defends her. "She is nasty!"

"She doesn't deserve to be married."

"Why would he pick her? She sins!"

Yet, with tears in her eyes, the bride keeps walking towards the groom who stands there with his hand extended, his eyes locked on her, and a smile that says, 'I hear them, but I'm still here waiting for you to join me.'

Then, the groom looks directly at you and his smile fades. His countenance becomes a question that says, "will you join them and also throw insults at my bride?" You nod in the affirmative. You want to warn Him and protect Him and even stop Him from committing to the wicked, nasty bride. But, before you can get a word out, you look around and realize the groom is Jesus and the bride is you.

Drop your weapon.

Many often read the passage about the woman caught in adultery and focus on the fact that Jesus wrote on the ground and said, whoever is without sin, cast the first stone. Very few would recognize that Jesus was giving a subtle reminder of the law that the eyewitnesses must be the first to execute the death sentence.

Whether Jesus was writing out that law or writing the specific sins of everyone present, remains a mystery. What I want to point out is that Jesus' actions in this moment not only saved the woman who was about to die by herself for something she was accused of doing with someone else, (That's another message), but also saved them from doing something heinous and criminal they would regret.

Some of you have been there. Ready to join the crowd and pass judgment on someone else. I can admit that I'm one of them who Jesus interrupted my judging and criticizing and stopped me from hurting someone who instead needed to be forgiven.

As we grow into the heroes that God has called to bring bold faith into this broken world, we must also drop the stones we have prepared to throw at those who have harmed us or those we simply dislike or disagree with. We are the 'them' that represent the bride that comes to the altar guilty of sin and yet the Bridegroom, Jesus, takes us by the hand to be with Him forever.

Prayer –

Daddy, thank you for your gracious love and kindness towards me. Remind me, in my weakest moments, that I am not perfect and that You forgive me and because of that I should forgive others. Bridle my tongue from gossip and slander against others. Open my heart to forgive and to speak grace and love to those who stand in need. I ask these and all things in the precious name of Jesus. Amen.

Reflect –

What do you hear God saying to you through this reading?

Change Reaction Challenge –

Your challenge is to start reading a Bible plan. The '1 of Them' plan on Youversion is a great plan but select one or more that speak to the season you are in now. The key thing is to grow closer to Jesus through God's word.

DAY 5:
Dealing with Failure

2 Corinthians 12:9 (NIV)

But he said to me, "My grace is sufficient for you, for my power is made perfect in weakness."

I started a business five years ago with a partner I'd known for years. We practically ran and built a company together and thought we were the perfect duo to start our own thing. The plan was solid, and we had a solid team and proven results of our effectiveness. I gave EVERYTHING I had to this business – my heart, time, and attention, my entire six-figure savings, and retirement. I sacrificed sleep, hanging with friends, and even seeing my family because I wanted to give this everything I had. When times became hard financially, I didn't hesitate to sell my jewelry and pawn my Rolex (a symbol and reminder of my previous success) to make sure that I could make payroll. There was no reason why this couldn't, shouldn't, or wouldn't work.

AND then the business failed, and I failed. I lost EVERYTHING, and I felt broken in a way I didn't know possible.

I was devastated.

Failure is one of the hardest things we have to deal with. We often end up being our own worst enemy. We blame and punish ourselves (whether consciously or subconsciously) for our lack of perfection, while we also pile on the added stress and pressure of over-analyzing the situation. Sometimes we even find ourselves at a point where we don't believe we're deserving of success and will wallow in our failure.

God grants us grace every day. Why don't we extend that to ourselves?

In 2 Cor 12:9, God reminds us that He is the only one that truly is perfect. Only He can make us strong where we are weak. He opens doors and provides the resources we need to win because only He can do that. It's not because of me, how hard I work or what I sacrifice, but it is because of Him that I can win the battles that I win and accomplish the things that I accomplish. Whenever I fall short, God fills the gaps. Failure is a natural part of life.

When I fail at anything, I do my best to remember:
1. Trust God to be who He says He is – He has never left, failed or forsaken us EVER, and that's because he's there. I am never alone.
2. Learn the lesson – Learn from the experience so that you don't have to learn it again. Learning makes us stronger and sharper.
3. Stand up, dust off and keep it moving – Life is a journey, and forward is the only way to go because there's more road ahead to travel.

Romans 5:3-5 says:

More than that, we rejoice in our sufferings, knowing that suffering produces endurance, and endurance produces character, and character produces hope, and hope does not put us to shame, because God's love has been poured into our hearts through the Holy Spirit who has been given to us.

Failure is an opportunity - it helps us rise to the occasion.

Failures help us to become who we're supposed to be, prepare us for what's ahead, and provide us with unique opportunities to learn and grow stronger. Failure doesn't define who you are, it's not your identity, and it doesn't mean that it's a pattern or your future holds the same result.

I'm more thankful for my failures than my wins, not only because I'm made better, stronger, and wiser because of them, but because I gain an opportunity to show others who God is and how he shows up in my life.

DAY 6:
Having Faith

We've all heard Hebrews 11:1 a million times, "now faith is the substance of things hoped for, the evidence of things not seen." But do we truly know how we exercise our faith? Too many times, we often find ourselves regurgitating words we've heard from our churches and pastors. It wasn't until my late 20's to early 30's that I realized what faith was. Faith is when God told me to quit my job and run my business full-time two months before the COVID-19 virus hit hard and businesses shut down. Faith is when God tells you a house is yours when there is already a contract from another buyer down on it. Faith is getting fired from a job two months before your wedding, and God tells you he has you and you end up not paying for a caterer, venue, or honeymoon. God wants us to be totally and utterly dependent on him.

There is no greater feeling than to rest in the Lord, knowing that he will genuinely supply all of your needs. I recognize that this is better said than done. It is so easy to praise God and trust God when things are going well, and every need is met in our lives. What happens the moment when you feel like you've hit rock bottom? What happens when all your bills hit you at once? What happens when your husband or wife loses hours from their jobs or loses their job altogether? What happens when you get sick and have no health insurance? God tells us to cast our burdens on him, and we still find a way to carry it ourselves. Take the leap and gain complete trust and confidence that our God has his children.

Let's not pretend like it's not scary to cast all of our cares on a man we haven't laid eyes on since we once were in heaven. We cannot pretend like we often pray to the Lord for help and get silence in return. It is easy to get mad with the most high when things look shaky. I will be the first to admit that I have been angry with God. When it feels like it's unbearable, and yet he told us in his word that he would not give us more than we can bear. The fact of the matter is God does not operate on our time. We also have to understand that we cannot pray for something, and in the meanwhile, we believe that it won't work because of our impatience.

Circling back to Hebrews 11:1, "now faith is the substance of things hoped for, the evidence of things not seen." We don't have to see it to believe what God told us. We don't have to see it to know that God had us before our foot even dashed against the stone. God will never forsake us. All he asks us to do is believe. Believe in the God we grew up to know from childhood to adulthood. God is not a man that he should lie. Do you want a new car? Do you want a new job? Do you want a spouse? Do you want more money? Do you want a new home? Do you want better friends? Do you want a six-pack or a flat stomach? Whatever you want, give it to God in prayer and know that your faith is on a level that you know God can and will do exceedingly above all that we can ever ask or think. I Am who I Am, says the Lord.

DAY 7:
Genealogy of Jesus

Normally, genealogies are the easiest parts of the Bible to skip over—many of the names are unfamiliar; thus, the significance of the lives of the people therein is lost. Recently, however, Matthew 1, which contains the genealogy of Jesus, has been a passage of my constant gaze and repeated reading.

David is the first person mentioned in the line of Jesus, which makes sense. Around Christmastime, we sing about how Jesus was born in the City of David, Bethlehem. And God said of David, "I have found in David the son of Jesse a man after my heart, who will do all my will" (Acts 13:22). Though he was the youngest of his brothers, God chose him to be king. He told Samuel His reason for rejecting David's older brother Eliab, "Do not look on his appearance or on the height of his stature, because I have rejected him. For the Lord sees not as man sees: man looks on the outward appearance, but the Lord looks on the heart" (1 Samuel 16:7, ESV). This is the type of person I would expect in the lineage of Jesus. He seems great! But what about the other parts of his life? What about the other people in this genealogy?

One woman who is mentioned is David's wife, Bathsheba. She's noted as "the wife of Uriah" (v. 6), meaning that David murdered Uriah so he could cover up that he slept with his wife (2 Samuel 11:14-17) and then took her as his own.

Tamar is another branch of Jesus's family tree. After God killed her husband Er and his brother Onan for their wickedness, she dressed like a prostitute and slept with her father-in-law, Judah. He had pledged that Tamar would marry his youngest son Shelah when he grew up, but fearing that Shelah, too, might be killed by God for being wicked, Judah didn't make good on his word. Therefore, Tamar took things into her own hands. When Judah was notified that she was pregnant, he wanted her to be burned for her immorality. Nevertheless, she revealed that she was pregnant by his own doing. Judah repented, and Tamar gave birth to twins.

Ruth is only one of two women to have an entire book of the Bible dedicated to her life. In this book, she is often referred to as "Ruth the Moabite." What exactly is a Moabite? Someone of the bloodline of Moab, a man born of an incestuous union between Lot and his eldest daughter (Genesis 19:37).

I found myself reading this genealogy in awe. Why would God pick these people to be in the royal lineage of Jesus—clearly broken and unworthy people whose lives were morally bankrupt? A liar who passed along the trait to his son (Abraham to Isaac), a murderer and adulterer (David), a feigned prostitute (Tamar), a real prostitute (Rahab), and a woman who was indirectly born of incest (Ruth)— I thought, These are the people You picked? They are. The message of the Bible has never been that God chose to use people because they were worthy or good; instead, He decided to use them because He saw what was inside of them; He saw that they believed Him. And from that belief, He made them worthy and good. No matter how broken your family or your own life may seem, the fact that God uses such flawed people in flawed families to tell so marvelous a story should cause you to marvel. If He can redeem a family tree so marred by sin, will He not also use yours?

DAY 8:
Faces of Fear

Fear has many faces, some helpful and others which are harmful. In today's world, we live in challenging times caused by a virus—COVID-19, affecting people worldwide. At one point, there was no cure or vaccine. We had reason to be afraid for our health and our very lives.

However, we cannot live in fear, and we have to choose not to allow ourselves to be overcome with fear. We have these precious promises from the scriptures: "God is our refuge and strength, a very present help in trouble. Therefore we will not fear, even though the earth be removed, and though the mountains be carried into the midst of the sea," Psalm 46:1-2. It sounds like it was written with us in mind today.

There are several definitions of fear. According to Webster's dictionary, they include:
1. A strong emotion caused by anticipation or awareness of danger;
2. Anxious concern;
3. Profound reverence and awe, especially toward God;
4. Reason for alarm--danger.

As you can see, fear can be helpful, i.e., if it prohibits us from participating in dangerous activities such as speeding, driving under the influence, or talking on the cell phone while driving.

Also, there is Godly fear - the reverence toward God, which we are commanded to have: i.e., Matt. 10:28b, "fear Him who is able to destroy both soul and body in hell," and Psalm 34:9, "Oh, fear the Lord, you His saints!" Another aspect of Godly fear that is comforting--"The fear of the Lord is the beginning of wisdom;" Psalm lll:10. Also, "Blessed is the man who fears the Lord;" Psalm 112:1.

However, there is the fear which may hinder us from moving ahead and receiving the blessings which may be just around the corner. This fear leads to inaction, perhaps because of a fear of failure--i.e., asking for a raise or just going job hunting. There may be a fear of the unknown or a fear of rejection. These are the fears we all may experience at some time in our lives.

There was a time when I thought I would never be able to drive in the city. Although I had a driver's license when I moved to Washington D.C., I let it expire. This was because of fear--the fear which cripples you. After about five years and two children later, I realized that I needed a driver's license. The policeman had mercy on me and passed me even though I couldn't park. Sometimes we avoid doing the very thing we need to do to enjoy life to the fullest.

The solution in my case was, the need for a driver's license was more significant than the fear of traffic. However, it's not always that easy. "For God has not given us a spirit of fear, but of power and of love and of a sound mind," II Timothy 1:7. This is the advice given by the Apostle Paul to Timothy, who he called "a beloved son."

We need to get from "a spirit of fear" to a "sound mind." This won't happen overnight, and we'll have to work at it. With God's help and our perseverance we will be able to conquer our fears. We're reminded in Proverbs 3:5-6, "Trust in the Lord with all your heart, and lean not on your own understanding; In all your ways acknowledge Him and He shall direct your paths." When we trust God to direct our paths, we will be on track to a sound mind.

DAY 9:
Power of Forgiveness

Psalms 78:38-39

Sometimes as Christian parents, we can forget that our children are just flesh just as we are. I had to learn this lesson the hard way. Having raised all of my children according to scripture and bringing them all up in a strict disciplinarian home, I did not expect them to be perfect, but I did expect them to live according to what they knew was right.

I was perplexed while having a phone conversation with one of my adult children, which left me bewildered by what she was sharing. She informed me that she felt that she had been traumatized coming up in our home. I initially thought the term "traumatized" was too strong, but later would have to agree that it was a correct use of the term, even though she admitted that she deserved most of the disciplines that she received growing up.

However, what she lovingly shared in our conversation was what she didn't receive. She stated that she felt she could not correctly love other men because, as a father, I had broken her heart. Now, no godly father would ever want to believe that their desire to love, protect and discipline their daughters would lead to breaking their child's heart. Maybe their spirit, but not their heart.

That phone conversation caused me too much consternation and introspection. However, after much soul searching, I came up blank. I knew I was a hard taskmaster, but I also knew I loved my children and that it was biblical not to spare the rod lest you spoil the child. For some reason, I could not put my finger on what I had done or not done to have warranted these darts to the heart.

In my brokenness, I finally reached out to the Lord in prayer, asking him to reveal a scripture that could bring some light to bear on my tortured soul. The spirit brought to my mind Psalm 78. At the time, I had no idea what was in this Psalm, and I just surrendered my spirit to read the entire chapter and waited on the Lord to speak to my heart.

After reading the entire chapter, I had my answer. Psalms 78 recounts the history of Israel's Exodus out of Egypt and God's subsequence disciplines along the way to Mount Sinai. It reminded me of the many disciplines I had extended to this one child. But it also revealed what I was sorely missing as a Dad. I was sorely missing what God brought to my attention in verses 38 and 39.

God was exacting my attention to look into his face, and all I could see was the face of a gracious father. God supernaturally led me to a scripture that showed him as a merciful father and showed me as a hard taskmaster. Something I was proud about now made me feel sorrow. It was a hard pill to swallow. I knew that I was a Dad who knew how to exact punishment for every infraction and then some. But now I felt remorse because now this exacting was the reason for breaking my daughter's heart. That evening, God broke something in me; something about his mercy and compassion awakened in me. God was carving a true image of a gracious father into my heart of flesh.

God was searing into my heart of flesh that he was still a compassionate God despite Israel, his adult children's stubbornness. He was branding in me that despite his adult children's sinfulness in the wilderness, he was still a forgiving God. My thoughts were being reshuffled as I read that he did not destroy them. Through my blurry tear-filled eyes, I was reading how instead of exacting punishment for each sin, he turned his anger away many times. My heart could not take this because that was not a part of my repertoire.

In conclusion, God opened my heart to see his motivation for all this. He knew that his adult children were only flesh and would disappear like the wind one day. Needless to say, I lay broken and sobbing, knowing that God was talking about adults, and I had laid all this wrath on a child.

There is nothing more rewarding than looking into the face of a gracious and loving daughter and know that you have been forgiven. It is also rewarding looking into the face of a compassionate, loving father and knowing that He has also forgiven you. Blessing be to God for his compassion, graciousness, and forgiveness.

DAY 10:
You Are the Church

Hebrews 10:24-25

I can still hear Granny yelling; it's time for church at 7 a.m., making sure we were on time for Sunday school. Can you remember those days? My family and I were the every Sunday crew. I loved it, but as I grew older, things changed.

You see, when you get older, some childhood traditions aren't forced on you anymore. I wasn't the every Sunday girl that I used to be. I felt terrible for not going to church all the time. About eight years ago, I gave my life back to Christ at the age of 24. I found an excellent church home and was back to the tradition I grew up with, which included going to church every Sunday, joining ministries, and attending young adult Sunday school. I was even blessed to teach a couple of Sunday school lessons. I looked up to so many people at my church, which is not bad, but I was putting people on pedestals. I had the wrong perception about the church and what God says about His church.

One Sunday, I missed church, and I had members calling me asking what was wrong because I wasn't there. I grew irritated because I wasn't feeling well, and I remember feeling like God was mad at me because I missed church. I don't know about you, but I put way too much pressure on myself by trying to be this perfect Christian woman. Let me tell you, I am not perfect, and neither are you. I don't know if you have been where I was before. You may have grown up like me and then drifted away from the church. You may be in a season where you haven't felt the urge to go back to church because of a bad experience you had. You may want to attend a church but haven't found the right one yet. Wherever you are, trust me, I get it all too well. I want to tell you something God shared with me.

YOU ARE THE CHURCH!

The church is a building that the Lord desires for His disciples, sons, and daughters to worship Him as one. Powerful things happen when we come together and fellowship. Having the Holy Spirit dwell in one place and transform people's lives is beyond words. There is nothing like it!!! Then, the Pastor will deliver a word that came from God, and your soul will be fed with clarity, knowledge, wisdom, truth, and maybe even confirmation. But God had to tell me that there is more to my walk with Him than just going to church. He told me, *"When you step out of that building you are a representation of me. You are the light that is walking around in darkness, and that light doesn't come from the church, it comes from me."*

You see, the church is just the meeting place for us. Nobody but us nurtures our relationship with Christ. Not your pastor, deacons, reverends, youth leader, or even your neighbor in the pew that sits beside you. God wants a genuine relationship with you, and it doesn't only happen at church. Your pastor is not responsible for your walk with Christ. They are only responsible for teaching you the gospel and helping you apply it to your life. You have to do the rest to become more like Christ and get to know Him. That includes taking what you heard on Sunday and meditating on it yourself, developing a prayer life, spending your own time with God, etc. The church cannot do that for you. You can have mentors to help you, but Jesus wants you and not just on Sunday! I used to make church a checklist. Thinking that if I go to church, God will be proud. Don't get me wrong; God wants us to fellowship with our brothers and sisters.

There is nothing wrong with going to church every Sunday. I encourage it, but I want you to look at it for what it is. It's a place where believers go to worship and learn about our Father in heaven. It is a place for healing. All of that will be with you when you leave those four walls-giving you the power and knowledge to spread the word and sprinkle Jesus wherever you go. Jesus is not just in the church, but He is omnipotent. Since we know that, we should show it all the time, not just in the four walls of the church. So, when the doors open back up to your church after this pandemic is over, I want you to run and worship the Father with your brothers and sisters. Enjoy having that divine connection with believers, but know this, you are the church. Even if you miss a Sunday or two, Jesus is still on the inside of you. You can worship Him wherever and He will meet you right where you are!

DAY 11:
Guarding Your Heart

Proverbs 4:23 (KJV)

"Keep thy heart with all diligence; For out of it are the issues of life."

The older I get, the more I understand how guarding my heart is key to my ongoing sanctification. One song that many of us sang in childhood rings oh so true. The song tells us to be careful little eyes what we see, ears what we hear, hands what we do, feet where we go, heart who we trust, and mind what we think. Why? Because the Father up above is looking down in love. So much good theology in a simple song. Proverbs 4:23 is an imperative verse that commands us to place great importance on our hearts. The New International Version starts the verse with "Above all else, guard your heart...."

We need to be like security guards when it comes to our hearts. Every time I go to work, I have to go through security. This process involves me taking off my coat, watch, lanyard, and purse and putting them on the conveyor belt to be x-rayed. In addition, I have to walk through a metal detector. Any metal will cause the alarm to go off. If the alarm goes off, I have to go through the second round of security measures which involves being checked with a metal detector wand. This process is done to prevent contraband or potentially dangerous items from getting into the facility. We need to watch over our hearts just as intently. What is meant by our heart? Is it the organ that beats in our body? This is true in the physical sense. However, in the spiritual sense, the heart is the center of our moral being, involving our emotions, desires and affecting our will.

Now is the time to take inventory of our lives and see if we need to turn contraband away at the entrance of our hearts that would serve to draw us away from our Lord. Let us review what we see, what we hear, what we do, where we go, who we trust, and what we think. Is there anything drawing us away from our Lord? If so, it is time to deny ourselves, take up our crosses, and follow Jesus. (Mark 8:34-38) He loves us immensely and paid the price for our sins. We owe Him our surrender and obedience. Let us run our race on this earth with a view to finish well and lay our crowns at the feet of Jesus when we see Him face-to-face.

Day 12:
Healing from Hurt

Proverbs 16:9 (NLT)

"We can make our plans, but the Lord determines our steps."

We had been married three years, and it was time to start a family. We had no problems getting pregnant the first time. Our first child was two, and we wanted to start on our second child. I was pregnant again and so excited to have another child on the way. One week from being three months pregnant, I lost the child. I made an appointment with my doctor to see what happened to the baby. He was out of town, so I had to see someone else. I was told to try to have another baby, but there was no explanation for why I lost the baby or any encouraging words to help with the loss. My mom said maybe something was wrong with the baby and the Lord decided to take it. We had told many people, so we had to return to them and say we had lost the baby. Everyone said they were sorry for our loss.

Isaiah 41:10 (KJV)

"Fear thou not; for I am with thee be not dismayed; for I am thy God: I will strengthen thee: yea. I will help thee; yea I will uphold thee with the right hand of my righteousness."

Well, we waited a while to try again after that. When I decided to try again, I got pregnant again and made it past the three months, so we started to tell people we were expecting again. A couple of weeks later, I had another miscarriage. It was the day of 9/11, and I decided not to go to work to have time for myself alone. I took a long walk because it helped me cope with going out in nature. I prayed to God to understand why did this happen to me again.

Ecclesiastes 3:1-4 (KJV)

To every thing there is a season, and a time to every purpose under the heavens: a time to be born, and a time to die; a time to plant, and a time to pluck up that which is planted; a time to kill, and a time to heal; a time to break down, and a time to build up; a time to weep, and a time to laugh; a time to mourn, and a time to dance;

Well, I tried to see my doctor to see what's was going on, and he was out of town again. I was told to try again to have another baby by someone else. I knew my husband wanted more children, but this was becoming hard for me to bear. He wanted to have a son, so I decided to try one more time. I wrote in my journal and read many Christian books on having miscarriages. Also, I needed another doctor because the one I had was not compassionate enough for me. I prayed about finding another doctor, and found one around the corner from where I lived, and I started to go to him.

James 5:14 (KJV)

"Is any sick among you? Let him call for the elders of the church; and let them pray over him, anointing him with oil in the name of the Lord"

I was pregnant again, and this time my husband and I went to our pastor to pray over us. When we were in his office, he said nothing was wrong. He put oil on me, prayed over me with his wife and another pastor.

My new doctor told me to get off my feet and rest every day

when I got off from work, and I carried my second child till term. I just needed to be still.

DAY 13:
When Hope brings you to your Calling

Romans 8:28 (TPT)

"So we are convinced that every detail of our lives is continually woven together to fit into God's perfect plan of bringing good into our lives, for we are his lovers who have been called to fulfill his designed purpose."

House mom and house dad.

That is the name my first set of foster parents acquired me to call them as I grew up. This is a distinct difference from the images that I saw on the TV screen. It was not abnormal to not have a father present in the communities where I grew up. But to not have either made me feel inadequate and irregular.

As I went through grade school, I was ferociously bullied due to the lack of material assets compared to my schoolmates. It wasn't hard for them to tell which kid was recycling the same set of clothes for school every week and which kid only had one pair of shoes that he wore every day.

I was different, which was the one thing I didn't want to feel. I thought, "If only I could be like everyone else. Have a lighter skin tone. Nice shoes. Cool clothes. A stable family. Maybe then, the cool kids wouldn't bother me." But by the age of 9, when I was finally adopted, most of the damage was already done. I grew up feeling like I didn't belong, like my life was hopeless. I thought I had no purpose, and I constantly had suicidal thoughts running through my mind.

By the time I went to high school, I was fed up with the world & I began to fight back. I did what any sensible teenager would do in this situation (sarcasm). I turned to the streets for the love that I lacked. I started to engage in neighborhood rivalries, which my school administrators often referred to as "gang violence." I was jumped, involved in street fights, shot at, and continuously put myself in life-threatening situations. I had nothing to lose but the purpose that God deeply embedded in me.

After getting kicked out of school for the 3rd time, I chose God wholeheartedly. I left the past behind and sought to follow after him. It was initially difficult because I had to believe in what I couldn't see. I believed that God could make things better despite what they were, and he did.

I took my GED exam and passed it easily. I went to community college right after that with no vision for my life, and God gave me one as he revealed my calling. I started to join the theater programs at my school, and my teachers loved me. This began to build my confidence and faith more in God. I graduated from Prince George's Community College and excelled at Towson University. Fast forward three years later, and I booked my first TV show called "Double Cross," which broke all of the viewership records on the network.

Matthew 18:12 (NKJV) asks, *"What do you think? If a man has a hundred sheep, and one of them goes astray, does he not leave the ninety-nine and go to the mountains to seek the one that is straying?"* My answer to that question would be yes; he would. God did that for me, so I know he will do it for you too.

Psalms 27:10 *(KJV) "When my father and mother forsake me, then the Lord will take me up."*

DAY 14:
Dark to Light: Finding Direction and Hope in the Trenches

It's striking how hopelessness slips into your life. The longer it lingers, the stronger it becomes. As a young mom to four children, my sense of hope dwindled early and fast. My husband worked the night shift for twelve hours or more almost every day of the week, with his days off often dedicated to catching up on sleep or completing college courses and the day being his time to sleep. So that meant I was the primary caregiver to our children 24/7.

Motherhood is one of the most cherished roles in my life, one that I feel God has called me to with my whole life being my preparation. However, my vision did not include long days and long nights by myself. It's hard to see the light when all you see around you feels like darkness. I was in the trenches for years, in the midst of the storm. This was not my vision, and this couldn't have been what God called me to.

Chronic sleep deprivation was my constant. Post-partum depression and multiple pregnancies ravaged my body. I was broken and breaking further. I spoke with my older brother about the difficulties of parenthood. He listened and calmly said, "It will get better, though." "What!?" I sat dumbfounded, mulling over his words. That night I realized that I let the struggles of life chain me down. I forgot that my circumstances could improve, and I could only see my problems.

Several months later, I hit another low point. One morning I sat on the living room sofa with a child who had trouble sleeping. The night before felt short and arduous. I was shocked that the sun was back up so quickly. As my head was reeling from the extreme exhaustion, I asked myself, "How am I supposed to do this?" Somehow, I found myself on a popular video streaming app. That morning, the first video that popped up was a Christian music video. I clicked on the app, and the first words were, "Not by might, not by power, by Your Spirit God." There was my answer. The words from Zechariah 4:6 left me paralyzed. I was reminiscent of the Israelites in Exodus 13, but I was traveled by night with no pillar of fire to light the way and no cloud by day. I forgot that I find my way through the darkness by looking to the God Who IS light, and in Him, there is no darkness (1 John 1:5).

At that moment, and the next moments after, I made a conscious decision to acknowledge my position in existence compared to the God of the universe. I was in the trenches counting my problems. God has counted the stars and knows them all by name (Psalms 147:4). My odds are better with Him. Parenthood is hard, but that does not mean I made the wrong choice. I had to remember that it is *"God is working in you, giving you the desire and the power to do what pleases Him"* (Philippians 2:13, NLT). That I needed to be *"confident of this, that He who began a good work in you will carry it on to completion until the day of Christ Jesus"* (Philippians 1:6 NIV). I held onto my conviction that God called me to motherhood and that *"It was for this He called you through our gospel, that you may gain the glory of our Lord Jesus Christ"* (2 Thessalonians 2:14, NASB).

These verses floated around in my head for the next few months. I found myself standing on them daily, walking in them with every task of the day. God reminded me that *"Weeping may last through the night, but joy comes with the morning"*

(Psalms 30:5, NLT). I discussed my depleting mental health with others, and my husband and I started therapy. Eventually, I was able to sleep more. My husband could get a different shift and could provide domestic support. My kids grew and became more independent. The dark of night was over, and my morning came.

So, if you are in the day and your trials are over, breathe that morning air in deeply. Bask in that sunshine and thank God that it has come. If you are in the dark of night and everything seems dark, and you feel trapped, take a deep breath. Lift your eyes to the hills. Ask God to fight for you. Hold onto God's promises. *"Confess your sins to each other and pray for each other so that you may be healed. The earnest prayer of a righteous person has great power and produces wonderful results"* (James 5:16, NLT).

Find someone who will listen to you and support you. Catch yourself when you dwell on what's wrong. Instead, acknowledge it, feel it and then look to God Who guides you. There is no suffering God does not know. The cross proved that. So, remember that the same God Who knows each time a small bird falls values you far more and knows the number of hairs on your head (Matt. 10:28-30). God is with you. He is for you. He will fight for you.

Is. 43:1-2, BSB

1Now this is what the LORD says—
He who created you, O Jacob,
and He who formed you, O Israel:
"Do not fear, for I have redeemed you;
I have called you by your name; you are Mine!
2When you pass through the waters,
I will be with you;

and when you go through the rivers,
they will not overwhelm you.
When you walk through the fire,
you will not be scorched;
the flames will not set you ablaze.

DAY 15:
L.I.M.P. (Lust. Immorality. Masturbation. Pornography)

1 Kings 18:21, (ESV)

(21) And Elijah came near to all the people and said, "How long will you go limping between two different opinions? If the Lord is God, follow him; but if Baal, then follow him." And the people did not answer him a word.

These four sexual sins (among others) cause you to stray from the Lord in its simplistic form. They are first enacted from a mindset of not trusting God to be what He alone desired to be for you. Each one of these sexual sins will immediately display a "LIMP" (faltering or wavering) in how you walk with the Lord.

The scripture above in 1 Kings 18:21 isn't directly related to sexual sin, but it does indicate that there is a point in one's life where one has to know that their actions are either drawing them closer to God or away from God. A choice has to be taken NOW to show who's side you are on.

Looking at these four scripture references for each acronym in the word LIMP, we will see why anyone who actively participates in them will end up further away from a trusting and fruitful relationship with Jesus Christ and more into a downhill struggle to know the Lord intimately and be an example of a faithful follower of Christ to the world.

Lust:
1 Peter 2:11-12, NKJV
(11)Beloved, I beg you as sojourners and pilgrims, abstain from fleshly lusts which war against the soul, (12)having your conduct

honorable among the Gentiles, that when they speak against you as evildoers, they may, by your good works which they observe, glorify God in the day of visitation.

Immorality:

1 Corinthians 6:18-20, NKJV

(18)Flee sexual immorality. Every sin that a man does is outside the body, but he who commits sexual immorality sins against his own body. (19)Or do you not know that your body is the temple of the Holy Spirit who is in you, whom you have from God, and you are not your own
(20)For you were bought at a price; therefore glorify God in your body and in your spirit, which are God's.

Masturbation:

1 Thessalonians 4:3-5, NKJV

(3)For this is the will of God, your sanctification: that you should abstain from sexual immorality; (4)that each of you should know how to possess his own vessel in sanctification and honor, (5)not in passion of lust, like the Gentiles who do not know God;

Pornography:

Matthew 5:28. NKJV
(28)But I say to you that whoever looks at a woman to lust for her has already committed adultery with her in his heart.

After reading these verses, you may ask, "where's the hope for me if I'm already guilty of one or more of these"?

1 John 1:8-10 (The Message Bible)
If we claim that we're free of sin, we're only fooling ourselves. A claim like that is errant nonsense. On the other hand, if we admit

our sins—make a clean breast of them—he won't let us down;
he'll be true to himself. He'll forgive our sins and purge us of all
wrongdoing. If we claim that we've never sinned, we out-and-out
contradict God—make a liar out of him. A claim like that only
shows off our ignorance of God.

**Now you might ask, "Okay, well, now that I know I'm
forgiven, how do I begin to overcome them?"**

Here is an answer that will be very helpful in Galatians 5:16,
(NLT), which says, *"so I say, let the Holy Spirit guide your lives.
Then you won't be doing what your sinful nature craves."*

Let the Holy Spirit guide your life by filtering your thoughts
to be more Christ-centered because your thoughts control what
you feel and what you feel is followed up by actions. Your actions
create relief, and relief breeds contentment and contentment forms
habits and can either become your burden or your blessing.

Philippians 4:8, (NLT)

DAY 16:
Navigating Obedience

Ephesians 5:10-17

Growing up, I remember going on road trips with my family. My dad would start the trip driving, and my mom would be in the passenger seat with a crucial task for the trip: reading the map that we kept in the glove compartment. Years later, printing out directions from online direction websites became the new norm. This was much easier than previous tracking lines with a marker of routes and highways, using a map big enough to cover the front windshield. I celebrate technological advances because those printed directions were better, yet not the best. If you missed a turn or got confused by the directions, streets you were on, or unpredictable detours, you were out of luck behind the wheel.

Today, we should all be grateful for GPS navigations systems on our smartphones. They are a lifesaver if you are like me and have a horrible sense of direction! Simply plug in the desired address and let the navigation system do all the work. And when you miss a turn, no worries: "Re-routing" your GPS will often tell you. If you follow what the GPS showed you, you likely would have gotten to your destination, having avoided accidents, avoided speed cameras, and reached there in the fastest way possible.

Isn't that what God's Word offers us? The opportunity to reach our destination or destiny if we follow what it says. The chance to avoid mistakes and crashes if we follow the Word. Warnings of traps ahead that we would not know about because they are hidden and in unfamiliar territory. Reaching places in life just at the right time because we followed the instructions. As great as my GPS navigation system is, how much better is God's navigation system: the Bible for my life? The instructions are clear, turn the volume up on the Word and follow what it says, then prepare to hear "You have arrived at your destination."

Prayer: God, help me trust in Your Word and Your voice. Help me trust you know the best route to take as you speak through the Bible.

Takeaway: The highest form of worship is obedience.

DAY 17:
Theology of Netflix

There are so many experiences that act as wells we can draw from for wisdom and perspective when we inevitably find ourselves needing greater context to build understanding. Sometimes those experiences for me come through casual Friday afternoons binging Netflix.

Derek Shepherd is a doctor. Many of you may know him from the series "Grey's Anatomy," which is also where we first met. I love doctor shows and was first drawn in by the "Good Doctor," which I couldn't find on Netflix, so I moved on to the Night Shift and haven't looked back since.

I watched a particular episode of "Grey's Anatomy" where the patient was experiencing extreme pain post opt. His mother was also present in the room, and it looked as if they were both regretting taking the risk of surgery though the post-opts pain was foretold in great detail. Derek first went to the patient to help remind him that pushing through this pain would allow him to have the life he dreamt of becoming a reality. Then he walked over to his patient's mom to provide perspective to her as she looked over at her son and found herself not in a position to help ease his pain. We might be able to imagine even the pain she was in emotionally at that moment.

Yet, with apparent confidence, Dr. Shepherd explained to the patient's mom that the pain her son was in was not unto death, but it was, in fact, the pain of healing. As patients ourselves, it's often difficult to distinguish the two because, for many of us, myself included, pain can often be perceived as inherently harmful, a sign of impending danger, or simply a cause for fear. I think if we were to ask our doctor, he would explain that there is a difference.

Many times as God is realigning our lives back into the original design according to His good and perfect will, we can often feel like patients on an operating table. However, we can find hope as we grow to understand that what currently is causing significant pain will result in the healing of so many areas of our lives.

If you look back in previous seasons, can you trace how the discomfort and pain may have been a sign of healing and recovery that resulted in greater strength in the next season?

DAY 18:
Power of Parenting

Depending on where you are in life, parenting may or may not even be on your radar.

But if you're planning on children being a part of your future, you're in for . . . a journey, shall we say!

And if you've already started down the path of parenting, you already know what we mean. A special shout-out to all the single parents who are on the grind every day supporting their children. And let's not forget the parents holding it down in blended families.

There are many "being a parent" scenarios. However, we've had the pleasure of serving newlywed couples in ministry for more than a decade. And when we encounter a newlywed couple with plans to have children, this is what we encourage: *be intentional about margin.*

What do we mean by that? We mean planning to make margin in your life to parent. Make margin regarding your time, finances, and focus. We encourage couples to choose to plan for that margin *before* children come along because it's crazy hard to create it after the fact.

The world somewhat paints becoming a parent as simply part of the life journey you can squeeze in among your other life goals, and it'll all just work out. But becoming a parent is way more than that. Becoming a parent is an honor granted by God and a responsibility to His Kingdom.

Psalm 127:3-4 (NIrV) tells us:

*Children are a **gift** from the Lord.*
*They are a **reward** from him.*

Children who are born to people when they are young
*are **like arrows** in the hands of a soldier.*

Gifts. Rewards. Arrows. You treasure gifts. You are honored to receive an award. And you carefully and intentionally aim arrows *if* you plan for them to hit a target successfully. That's not an easy task. Ask anyone who excels in archery; it takes skill, effort, time, and commitment.

It's challenging to take on the God-given assignment of raising children if your life is packed full—packed full of your career; packed full of bills, and a lifestyle that requires both parents to work "all the time;" packed full of all your personal interests and goals that distract from purposeful parenting.

Don't get us wrong. We're not saying that parents should drop everything and build their lives completely around their children. In fact, we discourage that! Christ should be at the center of your home, with your marriage as your first priority. But we see too many young couples who save no margin in their lives for parenting. So they have to "squeeze it in" between everything else. And they become frustrated and overwhelmed by the responsibilities of parenthood.

Consider each day as a plate. There's only so much room on the plate. If you keep piling food onto your plate, eventually, items start spilling over the edges and falling to the ground. And in life, usually, the things that get pushed off the plate are the very things we say we value most: our spouses and our children.

So keep in mind that you will need to have or make margin to parent your children well as you move forward in life. When God gifts you with a child, He has chosen you to fulfill a particular purpose as a parent. Don't miss out on what God would have you be in your children's lives because you're "busy." Make the margin. You won't regret it.

DAY 19:
Maintaining Mental Health

Matthew 1:18-25 (ESV)

18 *"Now the birth of Jesus Christ took place in this way. When his mother Mary had been betrothed to Joseph, before they came together she was found to be with child from the Holy Spirit.* **19** *And her husband Joseph, being a just man and unwilling to put her to shame, resolved to divorce her quietly.* **20** *But as he considered these things, behold, an angel of the Lord appeared to him in a dream, saying, "Joseph, son of David, do not fear to take Mary as your wife, for that which is conceived in her is from the Holy Spirit.* **21** *She will bear a son, and you shall call his name Jesus, for he will save his people from their sins."* **22** *All this took place to fulfill what the Lord had spoken by the prophet:*

23 *"Behold, the virgin shall conceive and bear a son and they shall call his name Immanuel"* **(which means, God with us).** **24** *When Joseph woke from sleep, he did as the angel of the Lord commanded him: he took his wife,* **25** *but knew her not until she had given birth to a son. And he called his name Jesus."*

Do you think Joseph had a hard time sleeping after that? I would have!

As a counselor, I see a surge in clients who are suffering from anxiety and sleep deprivation. Our sleep controls our circadian rhythm and our sleep drive. Our circadian rhythm is a 24-hour cycle that is affected by light. During adolescence, a natural shift occurs in the circadian rhythm that already makes a teen want to stay up and sleep later. However, teens have a growth spurt in their brain and emotional development and need up to 10 hours of sleep each night! Light from technology adds to the shift and delays going to sleep even more. We are now adding online learning to an already overloaded screen time schedule, and that constant light is affecting our sleep.

In addition, our sleep drive increases throughout the day. The longer it has been since we last slept, our sleep drive is stronger. However, anxiety masks our sleep drive and keeps us from a good night's sleep. Have you ever been up most of the night worrying about a meeting or a test that was the next day? Our lives are currently full of uncertainty. Young people report that worry prevents them from going to sleep and often do not share their worry with their parents because they see how stressed they are.

Anxiety occurs when we overestimate the threat of something, and we underestimate our ability to cope with it. Knowing who Jesus is helping us see that we are not alone as we cope with life's uncertainties. Immanuel means God with us! After recounting the death and resurrection of Jesus, Matthew ends his book with Jesus' words, "**I am with you always, even to the end of the age.**" With that, we can truly have peace of mind. Sleep well, my friend.

Some more helpful hints:
Know who Jesus is. Read God's word before bed.
Apps to download:
Abide
CBT-I Coach
Avoid light exposure and technology use the hour before bed.
Try not to nap, but if you must, not for more than 30 minutes or close to bedtime.

Go to bed and wake up at the same time every day. Many of us love to sleep until noon on the weekends, but this habit negatively affects our sleep during the week.

Do something relaxing before bed. Have a ritual that you follow.

DAY 20:
Peace of Mind

As a worrier since childhood, the Lord has taught (and is still teaching me) the blessing of having peace of mind. Though still an ongoing process, I have found the word of God to hold all of the solutions to my tendency to worry. He has provided all the spiritual tools and divine help that I need if I choose His way to have peace of mind.

The root of my worry is not trusting God fully and not believing that He will help me and give me the solution to my problem. Not trusting God meant that I, though a Christian, was walking in unbelief, not believing everything the bible says regarding worry.

There are many scriptures that I have learned to meditate on that help me when tempted to be anxious. I have memorized them, and God brings them to mind when I need help with some situation or another.

These are the times when I have had peace of mind: when I obey God's directive in Philippians 4:6, to *"be anxious for nothing, but in everything, by prayer and supplication, present your requests to God."* When I, through an act of the will and help of the Holy Spirit, immediately decide not to be anxious but instead turn to Him in prayer and petition, He indeed gives me a peace that passes all understanding and guards my heart and mind (Philippians 4:7). So, I have found prayer and believing by faith that "He is," is essential to my peace of mind. Disbelief and lack of trust in God and His provisions lead to the lack of peace of mind.

I ask God to help me to *"guard my heart with all diligence, for out of it are the issues of life"* (Proverbs 4:23). Since I do not always know how to do that, I ask Him to help me to guard my heart. The prayer of my heart is that God will *"create in me a clean heart, and renew a right spirit within me"* (Psalm 51:10). Confession of sin is one of the main ways that I know helps to stay clean before God, as 1 John states: *"If you confess you sins to God, He will forgive you your sins and cleanse you from all unrighteousness"* (1 John 1:9).

God has also shown me that my thoughts need to be monitored, shifted, and scrutinized by His Word. I ask myself if my thoughts are based on His Philippians 4:8 protocol of what to think on:*"… whatever things are true, honorable, just, pure, lovely, admirable, and of good report."* I also am learning the discipline of taking thoughts captive that does not honor God and to obey Him (2 Corinthians 10:5).

Peace of mind ultimately comes to me when I trust God, as He has directed in Proverbs 3:5-6: *"Trust in the Lord with all your heart, and do not lean to your own understanding. In all your ways acknowledge Him, and He will direct your steps."* As I offer up my body as a living sacrifice to God and endeavor not to conform to this world, He will transform me by renewing my mind (Romans 12:1-2). Jesus, the Prince of Peace Himself, stands ready to give us His peace (John 14:27). I rejoice that the Lord has given us access to *"…all that pertains to life and godliness"* (2 Peter 1:3) so that we may live victoriously for Him.

DAY 21:
Purpose of Perseverance

As we face many setbacks and trials in life, we have to decide never to give up on God's purpose for our lives. Perseverance means doing something despite the difficulty, and our trials are designed to build hope and character (Romans 5:4).

Instead of saying I give up, say, "What is God trying to teach me?" I learned this lesson through many setbacks. I was devastated when I was laid off from my job of 12 years. I didn't see it coming and wasn't prepared. I remember saying, '*I have a mortgage to pay and a child to take care of.*' After I got over the shock, I just trusted God to take care of me through this trial. I reflected on how he allowed me to save up enough money to live on for six months. He provided all my needs until I started to work again. My tribulation produced perseverance (Rom. 5:3). He taught me in this trial to trust and focus on him to meet my needs.

My spiritual life became stronger through this trial. James 1:2-4 reminds us to consider our trials as joy because it tests our faith, developing perseverance. Our perseverance must be made perfect so that we are complete and lacking nothing. God had another purpose for my life, and He transitioned me into another career sooner than I anticipated. God's timing is always right on time. Throughout the years. I have learned to continue to trust him with my finances, and he has never let me down.

When times get tough, you should remember to never give up on God's purpose for your life. Blessed is he who endures (James 5:11). This verse describes the perseverance of Job. Think about Job, who the Lord allowed Satan to test. Satan killed all his sons and daughters. How many of us could survive that? After losing all of this, he just worshipped God and said: *"I know that you can do everything, and that no purpose of Yours can be withheld from You"* (Job 42:2, NKJV).

Matthew 6: 25-34 reminds us not to worry. What does worrying do? It makes you lose sleep, unable to focus at work, and not want to be bothered by others. Worrying does not solve the problem; it makes it worse because you cannot stop thinking about it. God's word says, why do we worry? If he is going to take care of the birds in the air, aren't we more valuable than them (Matt. 6:26). Instead of worrying, we need to talk to God about our problems through prayer (Philippians 4:6). Talking to God is like talking to a counselor. You get it off your chest, and it makes you feel better. When we stop worrying and give it over to him, the Lord promises that he will give you peace that we cannot understand (Phil. 4:7).

The next time you face a trial that seems so overwhelming and you want to give up, push through it by giving it over to God. Let go and let God. Be confident that he who began a good work in you will carry it on to completion (Phil 1:6).

Day 22:
Premarital Sex (The Wait)

Galatians 6:8-9 (NLT)

"Those who live only to satisfy their own sinful nature will harvest decay and death from that sinful nature. But those who live to please the Spirit will harvest everlasting life from the Spirit. So let's not get tired of doing what is good. At just the right time we will reap a harvest of blessing if we don't give up."

I recently watched an episode of "Martin" where Gina, Martin's love interest, cooked Thanksgiving dinner for the first time. Despite the chaos between the two families, Gina managed to get a whole turkey in the oven. Gina removed the turkey from the oven at the end of the episode. It looked incredible! It had a nice golden color on the outside and looked like it was ready to eat. Unfortunately, that wasn't the case.

With the intent to carve the turkey for all to enjoy, Gina's father's single cut into the main thanksgiving dish caused it to bleed. Although it looked good on the outside, there was a problem on the inside.

The dish came out of the oven uncooked.

Don't discount your "oven time" or your singleness as most understand it. Outside of marriage, sex only satisfies that sinful nature, and sin always wants more of what it can't have. I chose to wait until marriage to have sex with my wife, and although it was one of the hardest things I had ever accomplished, it was worth the wait. It's worth waiting while God shows you where you need work, it's worth waiting while you enjoy that intimate time with the Father, it's worth waiting while He perfects you in the oven for the spouse just for you, and it's worth waiting to have sex until marriage.

Why? Because "At just the right time we will reap a harvest of blessing if we don't give up" (v.9). Stop worrying about you're getting too old to have kids; stop worrying about choosing a specific person so your kids come out with good hair, stop worrying about if there are any more good men/women left for you. Allow God to "cook you to perfection" by keeping you in the oven and adding every spice needed to make you the absolute best meal, so when it's time for you to emerge from the kitchen, you'll be a dish worth waiting for.

Through your faithfulness and focus on Christ, your blessing will come at just the right time if you don't give up.

Day 23:
Purity is Possible

Psalm 119:9 (NLT)

"How can a young person stay pure? By obeying your word."

Webster dictionary defines pure as: "free from anything that weakens or pollutes; containing nothing that does not properly belong; free from moral fault or guilt; marked by chastity (clean, spotless)." Purity is the state of being pure.

When you read the definitions for pure/purity, a sense of hopelessness could be the natural reaction. As a human being who has been alive for more than two years, chances are you are less than pure. Several things make it difficult for a young person to stay pure. For example, young people don't have the wisdom or maturity to make the best choices. Young people often put themselves in compromising positions, and when things go too far, they don't have the courage to stop. Sometimes young people have access to more money and freedom than they are disciplined enough to handle. A big reason is often their need to be accepted by their peers. I believe the most dangerous and effective reason purity is at risk is that young people don't have a solid grasp of Truth or effective strategies to apply the Truth they know.

Purity is not the only consideration for how to behave in sexual situations. I believe that authentic purity is a lifestyle and worldview that refuses to entertain vulgar, offensive, inappropriate influences in all areas of life, including what you listen to, what you watch, what you talk about, what you do, and where you go.

So, how does a young person keep their way pure?

I think it is possible to live a life of purity. First of all, I believe it takes a desire to want to live pure, which comes from having a solid personal relationship with the Lord that is vibrant and dynamic. This is not just going to church or saying a prayer when there is potential trouble. A dynamic relationship is marked by a passion for the Word and consistent pursuit of Him, not because you want something, but because He is appealing to you. You want to get to know Him better. Daily reading of Scripture has value. Add to that, asking the Holy Spirit daily to make Truth operational in your real-life and meditating on Scriptures to allow the Holy Spirit to show you how they apply to you specifically. It is also vital to get into a mentoring relationship with an older, more mature believer for accountability.

Doing those things will go a long way in helping a young person keep their track pure. There are some practical things that young people should practice also, such as not spending extended periods alone with a member of the opposite sex in secluded places, avoiding listening to and watching provocative media, don't go long periods of time without reading the Bible, and being in fellowship with other more mature believers. Make it a habit to keep short accounts with God – confess and repent immediately of all sins.

Nothing is fail-proof, so be willing to give yourself grace when you miss the mark but don't excuse yourself or justify your failure. Agree with God that it is a sin, and turn away from it and toward Him, His Word, and His people. I believe this is the best for a young person to keep their life pure.

1 Corinthians 10:13 (NLT): *The temptations in your life are no different from what others experience. And God is faithful. He will not allow the temptation to be more than you can stand. When you are tempted, He will show you a way out so you can endure.*

DAY 24:
Racism: Not Our Fault, But Our Fight

Racism is an issue that has plagued this world for centuries. It has caused division and separation. It has fueled anger, hatred, discrimination, and oppression. It has produced elitism and feelings of superiority among races. Above all, it has caused the world to disobey the second, and one of God's greatest commandments, as stated in Matthew 22:39, "... 'Love your neighbor as yourself.'

In Acts 17:26, we learn that God created every nation of man from one blood. No matter our race, we are all descendants of Adam. God made us in His image, and He never desired for us to dislike or despise another human being because of the color of their skin. Racism is not only a social issue, but it is a heart issue; it is learned, and it is a sin. As the traumatic deaths and events of 2020 continue to unfold, the last thing any of us can do any longer is ignore racism.

So as Christians, what is our response to racism? First, we have to "call a thing a thing." Racism is sin. 1 John 5 says, "*All wicked actions are sin . . .*" Wickedness is the equivalent to unrighteousness, and God calls us to be righteous. We grant God access to healing us from it by acknowledging sin. We also allow space for the forgiveness of those who have offended us and for ourselves if we have offended anyone. Forgiveness is the key to racial reconciliation.

Intentionally form relationships with people who do not look like you, and this will help you discover how much you are alike. Ask God to present you with the opportunity to connect with individuals you aren't familiar with on a deeper level. Be willing to have open conversations and dialogue about racism. Be prepared to ask and answer difficult questions and learn from the experiences of others.

Proverbs 31:8-9 states, *"⁸Speak up for those who cannot speak for themselves; ensure justice for those being crushed. ⁹Yes, speak up for the poor and helpless, and see that they get justice."* God does not want us to be silent regarding racism, and He wants us to speak up for those who are experiencing it. He wants us to do our part. Pray about the direction you should take regarding using your voice to speak out.

As difficult as it may be, God calls us to pray for our enemies and those who persecute us. Even if you are not directly being persecuted, still pray for the hearts of the individuals who choose to persecute. Consider those who are being persecuted and put yourself in their shoes. Pray to be educated if you lack knowledge in regards to their plight. Pray for a heart of compassion, empathy, and understanding.

Racism may not have started with us, but we have the power to do something about it. Take a risk and be a part of the change, not only for this world, but for the Kingdom of God.

Racism may not be our fault, but it is our fight! Start by being the change that you want to see in this world.

Prayer: God, thank you for equipping me with the power to fight and reconcile racism. Search me and show me anything that is not of You. Show me areas in my life and people that I need to forgive. Give me the strength and capacity to forgive even when it's hard. When I can forgive, I will move forward in reconciliation. I pray that I seek You before I take any action and give you clear direction and order my steps. Show me how to act, educate, listen and receive from a place of love. Give me the desire to be intentional about the relationships I form and the courage to speak up when I witness injustice. Equip me to be the change I want to see, not only for this world but also for Your kingdom. In Jesus' name. Amen!

DAY 25:
Receiving Restoration

We often ask for restoration when we're tired and weary. Often we feel like life has beat us down to the point where we can't even pray for ourselves. Usually, when we are at that point in our lives, we feel weak, lost, scared, and possibly even angry. We may be angry with God, ourselves, or even the world. This is the point where we need to dig down deep and muster up enough strength to pray for ourselves and even for others.

Job lost everything that he loved and cherished. Job lost his children, servants, crops, and even his animals. He was even inflicted with a horrible skin disease. Job was rebuked by his wife and even accused of doing something to deserve this suffering by his friends. Job became angry and began to question God and his character and demanded an answer from God. When we suffer, or something terrible has happened in the world that we can't understand or explain, we turn to God for answers, sometimes even blaming God.

As humans, we often believe that bad things shouldn't happen to good people, but that isn't the case. God didn't give Job an answer, but He does show Job the complexity of running the world and the universe. The world we live in isn't designed to prevent suffering. God doesn't promise there will be no suffering, and He never said that only bad people would suffer. He guarantees that we will endure some suffering in our lifetime.

And after you have suffered a little while, the God of all grace, who has called you to his eternal glory in Christ, will Himself restore, confirm, strengthen, and establish you. 1 Peter 5:10 ESV

God approves of Job's wrestling. Job brought all his anger, grief, and raw feelings to God. God wants us to come to Him honestly with all of our emotions and pain and just talk to Him. We should process our suffering through the struggle of prayer. *When Job prayed for his friends, the Lord restored his fortunes. In fact, the Lord gave him twice as much as before! (Job 42:1, NLT).*

God didn't restore Job's fortunes as a reward for praying for his friends. God blessed Job as a gift. God asks that we trust Him and His wisdom when we suffer and to bring all our pain and grief to him.

Prayer for Restoration:

Hey sky daddy,
I humbly come to you today broken and alone.
I cry out to you, Lord, please hear my heart's cry.
Today I reach out to you as I have many times before.
Give me rest, Lord, and restore this tired child of yours.
The world suffers, and people live in fear and rage. How can I cope? How can I comprehend? Sometimes it's hard to hear your voice through the cries of my heart. But I'll trust you. Sometimes it's hard to see your light through all the darkness in the world.
But I'll trust you.
I come to you, not just for myself, God, but for all those that are in need of hope, strength, and encouragement.
Take away their fears and dry their tears.
You know who is struggling, and you know each one by name (say their name)
Please have compassion and mercy.
In Jesus Name, Amen.

DAY 26:
Shacking up

Growing up in a large family made me appreciate having my own space. We lived in a family home for many years where space was limited and having my own room was not an option. I often imagined growing up and having my own place and couldn't imagine ever having a roommate if I could help it. During my first year of college, I had three roommates. We lived in a quad and had a ball! But I became a resident assistant the year after and lived in a single room until I graduated.

Once I was out in the world in my own apartment, I appreciated living alone more and more. I figured I would enjoy it until I was in a relationship serious enough to warrant living together. I never considered marriage as a requirement for living together. After all, my mom and stepdad never married and lived together for almost 20 years. My aunt and uncle lived together for several years and had two children before they married. So as far as I was concerned, I could live with my significant other, and maybe that would help me determine if we should marry.

At the age of 27, I entered a romantic relationship that made me feel like this was it, and we could live together to see how it went. After dating for six months, we decided to move in together and continued to do so for five more years. During the sixth year, God spoke to me in a way that I had never experienced. I landed a job that allowed me to integrate spirituality into my work, which revealed the many ways in which I had fallen short in my relationship with God. I soon found a church home at First Baptist Church of Glenarden and jumped into Christian education classes because I was eager to know why I was backsliding and how I could get back on track.

In that time, God spoke to me through His word and my trusted counsel about my romantic relationship of six years. During that time, I was led to abstain from sex and to initiate living separately from my significant other. During that time, it became clear to me that living together clouded my judgment and allowed me to grow comfortable in a relationship that was not God's will. I recall some of my early conversations with my significant other about how I came to these conclusions, and as someone unsure about his faith, he couldn't understand. He even asked if I was choosing God over him, and I absolutely was! I was reminded that *"you shall love the Lord your God with all your heart, with all your soul, and with all your mind"* (Matthew 22:37).

My love for God grew greater than my love for any human, and I needed my life to reflect that love. It took me six months to end that relationship after God made it clear that I needed to do so. It wasn't easy, and it was extremely uncomfortable, and I carried guilt about how this would impact my partner. I constantly spoke to God in prayer and through journaling, and He kept me encouraged. I even began therapy with a licensed counselor who integrated Christianity into her work. God provided me with all the tools to pursue more of Him and less of me. I am forever grateful for how this change shifted the course of my life.

DAY 27:
Soul Ties

Many people go through life and only have a few people that stand out as memorable. Some have a natural ability to reconnect and pick right back up as if the world was simply on pause since the last time you spoke. For me, it was the relationship that was meant to be, or so I made up in my head. We had previously dated and had an intimate relationship on and off for almost three years. The two of us just flowed, never argued, always supported each other's endeavors, and were simply great friends. The chemistry carried into our physical relationship as well. However, there will always be an issue, no matter how great the relationship, if it moves beyond the boundaries God has set for you.

Much like your parents have boundaries to mold you as you mature, God has created boundaries to protect you. I Thessalonians 4:1-8 outlines the "Plea for Purity" for us to know how to control our bodies. Your draw to check in on the person from the past may be more than simple curiosity.

A soul tie is typically formed from an intimate or strong emotional relationship. By ignoring God's boundaries for a healthy relationship, I found myself emotionally connected with him long after our relationship had ended. Finding every excuse for us to be in the same room, check up on him on social media, or inquire with family with whom he still maintained a friendship. It took a very long time to realize that I was spiritually stuck on him.

All relationships after him were unsuccessful due to my inability to disconnect from him. The feeling was mutual as he reached out the same way, and we always found a way to be in each other's presence. He would reach out when I had him on my mind. God sent, right? Wrong. The spiritual connection is still present, and you have to ask God to release you from the stronghold. II Corinthians 10:3-5 makes it clear that "...though we walk in the flesh, we do not war according to the flesh. For the weapons of our warfare are not carnal but mighty in God for pulling down strongholds." I ask that you say this prayer to release you from any soul ties that remain in your life.

Dear God,
Thank you for being forgiving and allowing me the ability to learn from my past mistakes. I'm sorry that I have not treated my body as a temple in a way that honors you. I realize the power that can be manifested in maintaining a physical or emotional relationship with someone other than my spouse. Please allow me to move beyond the hurt and release the emotions associated with the person I am connected with spiritually. Allow me the ability to discern the intentions of those around me. Free me from the obsessive thoughts, social media check-ups, and lustful spirit. Protect and strengthen the communication, love, and bond with my spouse and remove the temptation that draws me to the past. In Jesus Name. Amen!

Scriptures:
1 Corinthians 6:18-20 (NKJV)
Proverbs 4:23 (NKJV)
1 Thessalonians 4:1-8 (NKJV)
2 Corinthians 10:3-5 (NKJV)

Day 28:
Stop Stressing

Isaiah 26:3-4, (CSB):

"You will keep the mind that is dependent on you in perfect peace, for it is trusting in you. Trust in the Lord forever, because in the Lord, the Lord himself, is an everlasting rock!"

I can honestly say that I have never really been one to stress out or spend a lot of time worrying about things. I'm not sure why but it never has been part of my DNA.

Until……2020 hit, and my life was rocked with a barrage of unexpected and unfortunate events. Have you ever heard of the saying, "life comes at you fast"? Well, life this year certainly awakened me to that saying. Even the wise Forrest Gump said, "Life is like a box of chocolates; you never know what you're going to get."

This year was surprised with losses in multiple areas of my life. From losing a loved one, losing financially, and losing some friendships, 2020 did not go the way I envisioned. Because of these unexpected happenings in life, I found it so easy to stress. I would stress over how much money was in my account, my future, and other people's opinions. Whatever you could think of, I found myself worrying about it.

What I had to realize was that my God was not a God of stress, and never once in his word had he commanded me to worry about a circumstance here on earth. I was so busy focusing on everything that had been going wrong that I had not focused on my heavenly Father, who can make all things right. Instead of focusing on how big my God is, I focused on how "big" my problems were. Instead of feeding my faith in God, I had been feeding my worry and stressing out. The verse from today's devotional says that the Lord will keep the person who is dependent on him in perfect peace. It also says that we can trust in the Lord forever because he is an "everlasting rock."

Once I started focusing on my word and tapping into who God is, I started looking at the trials I face in life differently. The more you know about who God is, the less worrisome the stresses of life become. Why worry about the things the world may bring when you serve a God who controls EVERYTHING!! Take time today to dive into God's word. Look at how faithful he has been throughout the ages. Get a glimpse of the God who has the whole world in his hands and make that decision today not to stress or worry, but to trust in the fact that God is in control!

DAY 29:
Temptation into Addiction

Temptation is one of the hardest things Christians face daily. Whether it's the temptation to lust after the opposite sex, smoke, drink, or something else, we all have our battles with temptation that is hard to overcome. Nobody ever said being a follower of Jesus would be easy.

In college, all my friends were either smoking, drinking, having sex, or doing something illegal to make money. It's cliché, but the saying "Tell me who your friends are, and I will tell you who you are" has truth to it. It didn't take me long to start doing the things I saw people around me doing. The thing about me is that I felt no conviction because I was making all A's and B's, but I was thinking about a different conviction. Since I was making good grades, friends and family wouldn't convict me about my lifestyle, but I should have been convicted by God about my actions because I didn't represent him.

After I graduated college, it got worse for me. Although I got blessed with a job right out of school in the same profession that I got my degree in, I started doing more things ungodly. My temptation turned into an addiction with things that weren't pleasing to God. I use to think, I'll do this now and then ask for forgiveness right after. Well, actions have consequences, and it hit me all at once, literally.

One night out with my friends, I drank too much, and while walking to the car, I passed out and fell face-first on the concrete. That moment ironically woke me up. So, I cut back on things that I knew wasn't pleasing to God.

After getting that career job right out of college, I somehow ended up working a regular job outside of my career field for about 5-6 years. I started feeling like I wasted my degree and was not fulfilling God's purpose for my life.

I started going to church more, joined ministries, started hanging out with people to keep me accountable, and even went back to school for my Master's degree. I had some slips up even after all that, but I felt the Holy Spirit working on me. I started seeing changes in my life that I never thought would happen.

In 1 Corinthians 10:13, it says: *"No temptation has overtaken you except what is common to mankind. And God is faithful; he will not let you be tempted beyond what you can bear. But when you are tempted, he will also provide a way out so that you can endure it."*

This verse made me feel more confident about my choices because no matter what temptation came my way, I knew I could handle it. Not only that, but God will provide me a way out of any situation I face, no matter how difficult it looks at the time. Whenever you feel like you are being tempted beyond what you can control, remember God is right there with you to provide a way out, and he knows that you can endure it.

Day 30:
The Holy Spirit: Divine Intoxicator

Eph 5:18

The most misunderstood element of the Christian life is the person of the Holy Spirit. He is like that strange cousin everybody knows is part of the family, but no one wants to talk about.

First, we must recognize the Holy Spirit is a person. He is not an "it" or "thing'. He is the third person of the Godhead. God the Father, God the Son, and God the Holy Spirit. He is just as much God as the Father and the Son. However, each person has taken on a different role and function within the Godhead. Our salvation was planned by the Father, purchased by the Son, and implemented by the Holy Spirit.

Jesus said, it is to your advantage that I go back to heaven, so that I will send the Holy Spirit to you (John 16:7).

Why is the Holy Spirit essential to our Christian life? He convicts us of sin and our need to accept Jesus (John 16:8). He is the one who regenerates us and makes us alive, new and born again (Titus 3:5).

In the moment of salvation, the Holy Spirit places us in the body of Christ (1Cor 12:13) and comes to live in us. Imagine, your body is the dwelling place of the Holy Spirit (1Cor 6:19, 20; John 14:17). He also seals (secures) us for eternity (Eph 4:30).

The Apostle Paul, in frustration, asked the Galatia Christians, "Are you so foolish? Having begun in the Spirit, are you now being made perfect in the flesh?" (Gal 3:3). If we could not be saved without the Holy Spirit, what makes us think we can live the Christian life with human effort? It can't be done. We need the Holy Spirit.

How the Holy Spirit enables us to live the Christian life?
The Holy Spirit leads, empowers and strengthens us (Rom 8:14; Acts 1:8; Eph 3:16). He enables us to live holy, giving us victory over sin (Gal 5:16; 2Cor 3:17; Rom 7& 8). He transforms us into the image of Christ (2Cor 3:18).

Some believe we need more of the Holy Spirit, and the truth is, we already have all the Holy Spirit we will ever get. The issue is not us getting more Holy Spirit, but the Holy Spirit getting more of us.

The Key. I am convinced the key to the Christian life is living under the control of the Holy Spirit.

Eph 5:18 "And do not get drunk with wine which is debauchery, **but be filled with the Spirit.**"

Notice these are commands, not suggestions; be not drunk, but be filled with the Holy Spirit. To be filled means living under the control of. Paul compares being under the control of the Holy Spirit with being under the influence of alcohol. In the same way, alcohol controls the intoxicated person; the Holy Spirit controls the believer. Alcohol controls emotions and mood, and it controls what they say, how they say it, controls their reactions, motor skill, and how they walk. The Holy Spirit controls what we say, how we say it, how we walk, where we walk, how we think and respond. He controls our moods and attitude.

Practical application. Living under the control of the Holy

Spirit means that <u>daily</u>, you and I voluntarily surrender control of our lives to Him.

Prayer "Holy Spirit, today I surrender control of my life to You. Help me to hear and be sensitive to Your voice. Lead me, empower me and convict me. I will listen and obey. Make me more like Jesus. Amen."